REBORN

REBORN

To heal. To believe. To love.

Amy Hsuan Chiu

NEW DEGREE PRESS
COPYRIGHT © 2019 AMY HSUAN CHIU
All rights reserved.

REBORN
To heal. To believe. To love.

ISBN   978-1-64137-304-3 *Paperback*
                978-1-64137-587-0 *Ebook*

For my brother, Tony.

Contents

REBORN: A book to heal   11

Part 1.   Embrace Moments of Darkness   15

Part 2.   Let the Light Peek Through   41

Part 3.   Say No Sometimes, Be Kind All Times   63

Part 4.   Fight Like a Warrior   87

Part 5.   Finale—Not the End   113

Work Referenced   119

Acknowledgements   121

Author Bio   125

"We don't read and write poetry because it's cute. We read and write poetry because we are members of the human race. And the human race is filled with passion. And medicine, law, business, engineering, these are noble pursuits and necessary to sustain life.

But poetry, beauty, romance, love, these are what we stay alive for."

—N.H. KLEINBAUM, DEAD POETS SOCIETY

Introduction

REBORN: A book to heal

Dear Dreamers,

Looking back, becoming a writer was inevitable for me. For a long period in my life, all I had was writing—and, more specifically, poetry. The existence of poetry took away my loneliness and somehow shared my pain while I was growing up.

When I was fifteen, I started writing using my pen name, Aeimee, and created a fan page on Facebook. I chose the name Aeimee because it sounds similar to my legal name, Amy. I did not want my classmates to find out I was writing at that time, so I purposely hid my identity behind the writing. I created the Facebook page as a space for my pieces, thinking no one would read them. Whenever I experienced hardship, I would put pen to paper and use writing as a medium to heal myself. After a few months, my page reached 3,000 readers, which was startling for fifteen-year-old me. I realized my readers were all around the age of thirty and had no idea about my age and identity. I felt the pressure to write "well," yet I wanted to be honest with myself, my texts, and my readers. I didn't want to write just to impress someone. I was real, and I kept writing.

As time went by, I began receiving inbox messages from strangers on my writing page. At this point, I learned the power of the words in my writing. The messages included sentiments such as "I was feeling down today, but I saw your words and they made me feel like I'm not alone. I could really relate to what you wrote about life. I hope you will keep updating." The power of such messages motivated me to overcome hardships in my life as well. Although I never met my readers in real life, I felt like I could connect and be with them through my words. These interactions marked the first time someone referred to me as a writer and the first time I identified myself as a writer.

After two years of writing as Aeimee, I got in touch with an editor. We discussed my Facebook fan page, and I told her I wanted to share my words with a larger audience. The editor worked for a growing platform called Womany, a female lifestyle website created by and for women in Asia. She explained to me that the platform looks for columnists and authors who examine different issues in society and offer encouragement for all women. I cried tears of joy because I became one of the youngest columnists on the site, with no one knowing my identity or that I was only seventeen. The readers followed because of my words, not because of certain "qualifications." It was amazing for me to see my articles being put in the same category as many senior authors in their thirties and forties whom I look up to.

I still post on the Aeimee Facebook page today, and I still get inbox messages from my readers saying they are looking forward to reading my updates. After nearly eight years of managing and writing on the page, I have learned the power of my poetry and words. I thought to myself: *I am ready to write this book.*

English is my fourth language. I find the rhymes and formation of words fascinating, especially when I first read William Shakespeare and Edgar Allen Poe. I handwrite poems and ideas in all the languages I know outside of school. Most of my short fiction and poetry are written in Mandarin and English, as are the articles I write for newspapers and columns I write for lifestyle platforms. But, deep in my heart, poetry is and will continue to be my favorite.

When someone shares their poetry with you, they might as well be showing you their naked body and a part of the soul. For many of us, we've been through too much and have become afraid. I feel the same fear. I realized writing a book that touches on personal matters and different emotions could bring back the past I wanted to forget. Yet here I am. I want to be real with my readers. I face my past experiences with courage and with my writing. Poetry is a way to heal. Living through depression, anxiety, bullying, language barriers, identity confusion, and a loss of self-esteem, I started to see the negative moments as a part that completes me. I have experienced both sunlight and shadows that people don't see.

I hope my first book of poetry brings you strength when you feel like you are fighting against the world. I will address my stories, scars, painful memories, regrets, and how I still manage to live with some of them even now. I want this book to be a gift, a tool, and a practice to remind you, me, and our loved ones the importance of the little moments and the simple joy in them. By the end of this book, we will remember to be kind to ourselves and to the world, despite knowing the harsh reality behind our dreams.

In the end, we are all people with stories. Some have good endings, and some have no resolutions. Those that don't work out are the reason I'm here to share my poems.

Love,

Amy Hsuan Chiu

Part 1

Embrace Moments of Darkness

The Small Talk

Let's talk about something meaningless
talk about the weather
have a nice day!
how are you?
Are we asking just to be polite? because of our
social values?
Who's going to ask?
how's your soul? and to listen?
Don't let the social structure decide how you are greeting
one
and another.

It takes guts to treat people kindly these days.

Be one of the first to spread the kindness.
Be one of the first to value the sincerity.

Humans

We humans.

Refuse to understand
Because we don't understand

We are humans.

Forgive when we can't forget
Leave when we can't forgive

We are just humans.

Remember the regrets with a full heart,
yet
come to realize the truth in details too late.

Grace behind not asking

Does he know that she loves you?
Does she know that she loves you?
Does he know that he loves you?

Do they know that I love her?
Do they know that you love her?

"Yes, I do."
It's none of *your* business.

Knot

Do not ever
tie people up with your own
knots from
the past.

Showing off the scars
Hurting them with wounds
Grown on your bare skin

It's their fault
for being unkind,
it will become
your sin if you
drag
people with malice.

You should be glad I'm alive

"Congratulations!"
You
are alive.
Those who pretend they cannot see are
officially blind as well.

"Congratulations!"
You
can only breathe.
This is the one characteristic of a
living man.

"Congratulations!"
You
are feeling.
Tones expressions faces voices
their eyes.

The gray joke the world makes and
oneself's dusty minor existence.

Congratulations.

Things

Those things that everyone wants
are not necessarily what everyone needs.

From their Mouths

"I want to have a stable job."

          "I want to be married to someone who loves
me deeply."

"I want to get a lot of money!"

          "I want to have seventeen cats in my apartment."

"I want to travel the world and discover myself."

Hey, I'm envious of you.

I just want to wake up,
in every, typical, ordinary, morning,
and be able to feel
a real, existing, existence of my physical
being,
feeling meaning, hopeful about
starting my day,
that is—my dream.

                              "I just want to
be happy."

                    —AHC

Only, If

If I had never met you,
I wouldn't be sitting here crying alone
I wouldn't be staying up all night looking over our old
photos
I wouldn't be hating myself for who I am when I am with
you
I wouldn't be dealing with rumors of those false stories
I wouldn't be feeling sorrow within me when I pass by
your favorite restaurant
I wouldn't be so jealous of the new girl standing next to
you
I wouldn't be so judgmental of every joyful thing in the
world
I wouldn't be questioning my sanity and having to go
through counseling
I wouldn't be skipping meals just because I no longer feel
the need for food
I wouldn't be losing control and dumping my favorite
apple juice into the sink again
I wouldn't be getting nightmares of drowning slowly with
you
I wouldn't be seeing the world with such a pathetic view
through blurry eyesight
I wouldn't be seeing rain as teardrops from God
I wouldn't be hating all the radio stations that play romantic songs
I wouldn't be doubting all other men who have brown
eyes similar to yours
I wouldn't be feeling like the world may collapse in the
next second

If I had never met you,
I wouldn't be sitting here writing this last line.

Netizens

To those living behind the keyboard,

watch your typing speed
one emoji, one sentence, one photo
that is how you take someone's life
away.

watch your killing sword
"people so ugly like you should go die"
"I wish your parents never gave birth to you"
"you're fat like a pig"

watch your blinking moment
log in, write a comment, log off
log in, edit a comment, share the post, log off
log in, tag a friend under a comment, share the post, log
off

... *is typing*

Your life is beyond the screen

The distance between your thumb to the screen
is much closer than the distance between you and
your loved one living in your chatroom

Torian

"Don't marry him."
"Why can't I?"
"Because he is Torian.*"

A cup of water full of stereotypes
will not be changed even if
it is put in the freezer
in the world we live in today.

"Torians all smell bad."
No, that's the smell of comfort
that reminds me of home
for the first time.

"Torians look down on women."
No, I know many Torians who
are gentlemen and kind to everyone;
women are never exceptions.

"Torians are selfish people."
No, you never trusted any one of them.
How dare you judge someone without
truly walking in their shoes?

How dare you?

I know a Torian, and I am proud
of him.

—

* Torian is a word made up by the author. The author does not write a specific race
because she does not want to limit different readers' experience.

The night of rain

Don't say cheer up to those
waiting in the rain for the ones
who left a long time ago.

We all live in the street that
can only fit in a certain amount of us
with a certain amount of sadness.

When it floods, some people still stand
there and enjoying being swallowed by
another endless night in the city.

You can try to drag one out, but you will
end up learning that they are voluntarily there
because they are still expecting a different ending.

What we know about Snow White

They talk about the beauty,
the innocence, and the patience.

No one goes to understand
what the witch truly desires
and what causes her pain behind
the poisoned apple.

To be saved is Snow White's talent;
would she have woken up if it wasn't a prince, but
a poor monster riding on a hairless donkey?

Happily ever after is not the end.
It's the beginning of what you do not want to
believe in after.

To be saved could be an option.
It's what happens next
that determines if she
deserves to be a princess.

I am

I am mad for you when you don't stand up
for what you believe

I am mad for you when you don't talk back
when they hurt someone you love

I am mad for you when you try everything
you could and are forced to quit

I am mad for you when you push everything
away to save your self-esteem

I am mad for you when you are treated
unfairly by daily life and today's bad weather

I am mad for you when you are not
mad at the way you are treated

I am mad for you when you are not
being honest and being kind
to yourself

Peoplephobia

Open the wooden frame door,
put your head down and let your long black
hair cover your ordinary round face,
walk straight to the dusty, comfortable corner
while doing the mobile order in its store.

I am a person with peoplephobia.

Take a sip of the Americano, praying no one
noticed how loud of a sound you make while
adjusting the shaky antique chair, again avoiding
the eye contact with the red-haired girl who
always sits next to the window on Wednesday afternoons.

I am a person with peoplephobia.

"How are you doing?" "...good."
Did my voice just shake? Was he disgusted by my pimples
and uneven smile? Did my breath smell? I live with these
enemy-like friends. They knock on my door sometimes
without giving a heads-up, rejecting all my vacation plans.

I am a person with peoplephobia.

Fish are better than us

One says the fish needs water,
knowing water doesn't need it.

Pitiful?
No,
it's the fish's courage that comes
with a choice.

Settling down in the same
temperature / environment / partner

That's the utopia we, humans, will
never

reach.

Marshmallow Prison

When he is small,
his father told him to stay in

the room. If he stays in for one day,
he gets to eat one marshmallow.

If he stays in for a week, he will
get to eat five times as much.

No one ever tells him who and what
gives his father the marshmallow.

The marshmallow factory is still
running and functioning,

creating more playrooms that
await to break the patience.

—

Inspired by Walter, Mischel. *The Marshmallow Test*. Transworld Digital, 2014

Like You, Like Me

I keep on waving,
"Look over here, please!"
Hoping that someone will notice

I keep on standing,
"I can be your umbrella!"
Auditioning to be the best guard in the rain

My tree trunk is thin and wrinkled
With skin color between yellow and white
Like yours, like mine.

My root is grabbing the soil tight
With energy given to me by nature
Like yours, like mine.

My body feels every clear drop of water
With freshness like a wakeup call
Like yours, like mine.

My arms long for a hot summer hug
With sincere care and love
Like yours, like mine.

I keep on posing,
"Am I good enough yet?"
Standing in front of the orange wall

I keep on thinking,
"When will anyone hear me?"

Trying to stand out among them
All I'm asking is that—one chance,
To be—someone's first priority

Like you, like me.

Bread or Love

They say young girls
sacrifice their youth to the
men they date when they are young.
But no one ever talks about the young boys
who spend an equal amount of time on the young girls.

They say women will choose
bread over love when they pass a certain age.
But no one acknowledges the ones chasing after time
and choosing their own, absolute self-confidence without
any shame in front of their old, worrying parents.

They say older women will definitely pick bread
over love because they are the leftover ones on the stock
that need to be out before the 10 p.m. closing time for
the bakery, forcing a choice on them and signing a paper
that does not promise a bright future or a loving, stable
balance of the two.

What's in Your Latte

Can I get a tall iced latte with 100 % pure kindness
and a shot of positive love?

Wake me up from the distance between
my dreams and the reality in front of the blue
metal office desk.

Let it echo. Praying that one day someone
will notice what is added on to the corner
when the dust piles up on someone's
shiny, bright forehead.

Ask the new interns to get us more lattes.
I will drink away the bad and the good,
staying all night by myself
and with you.

Before the storm

They shake hands with a smile at the dining table
no one pretends to know what is going on
when one of them leaves the table,
the other starts to talk about what has gone wrong
and ignore all the things that are done right

They sit down next to each other with a straight face,
thinking no one will find out what is on their minds
if they just keep on looking at the little blue screens,
making time go away by spending time together
and pretending this is just a normal gathering

They buy food and feed one another during every festival,
it's basic manners that they use to treat other humans,
making the ones who don't follow the routine the odd
ones, they expect and reach their arms out, asking for
more and more, the gifts are piling up, and they are still
waiting

People

people will be people they gather only when tragedy
happens I've tried all the sayings prayers to the family
God bless the hurt rest in peace like a handmade glass
candy jar shattering when dropped the red white marbles
someone call 911 we need backup officers here picking up
the rotten ones the suspect is firing people will always
be people those in suits and ties promise they will sweep
away the dust in the museum of history we believe and
we listen the media put a mic in front those *how do you
feel about losing your son* here I am waving the country's
dream regrets to see how quickly we forget I try to find
a cure to our Alzheimer's repairing those fragments of
sweets people will always be people in the end who is
to blame whose fault is it the system tapes the jar back
together we blindly see no cracks the lives gone are gone
forever there are things done that cannot be undone your
children are not your children but people will always be
people

Part 2

Let the Light Peek Through

Good Person; Bad Person

A real bad person does not lie.

The one who lies
is always a bad person who
is dying to be a
good person.

Oxygen

Watch,
the season has passed. I learn
nothing of my name. I write things
down. I sing a phrase & break it down
& the flower starts blooming.

"Why do you write?" people ask,
I hear the calling.

I write who I am,
I love whom I write for.

Mr.

Having someone by your side
An existence that is irreplaceable
Never worrying about the time that is gone

Knowing each other's every little habit
You & Me, sitting side by side, watching time go by
On time, delayed, it's fine.
Undeniable exchange between two souls

To someone who taught me to say
"I love you" in 365 different ways.

The Sparks

go out of the house,
take a step and travel to somewhere
long road, one path, green light

find out what makes you mad,
explore what makes you excited,
look for what makes you thankful

my dear,
what sparks your heartbeat is
what you should chase after.

Poetry is not like you

Poetry is not like you
It never lies

Poetry is not like you
Everything you feel here
is
what it is

Poetry is not like you
Everything you feel here
is
real

Poetry is not like you

01

You have all the options
in life, but you can't choose them all.

What does it mean to get peace
of mind?

It is to walk on the path
that makes you feel like
you belong, again.

Across the shades and shadows,
you've come this far—
to meet the best version
of you.

Goodnight

He likes to see the way she falls asleep. He, the thirty-year-old photographer, chooses to memorize the details of her with his eyes. She, the twenty-eight-year-old artist, is always there by his side to find inspiration.

"You know. There are moments that cannot be captured by cameras. Moments that are too worthy, too precious to be seen through camera lenses."

The LED string light is hung on her wall, lining up into a heart shape, and there are photos of her family and friends around it. *That says a lot about her personality, doesn't it?* he thinks to himself. It's the time of day when she becomes like a kitten and wraps herself with heavy, fluffy blankets. He then turns off the light and sees the warm string light reflecting on her face.

She closes her eyes as he sits on the bed's edge, his hand patting her back. Her cheek has the soft baby pink color that reminds him of a newly bloomed tulip in spring. *Oh.* Her silky hair lies there quietly. A sudden warmth flows up to his mind.

That's the moment. That's it. He loses himself in seeing the scene.

"Goodnight, darling."

He takes the teddy bear he bought her years ago and places it next to her pillow as if she is still a little girl.

From a Father to Daughter

To a father growing old, nothing is dearer than a daughter.

—EURIPIDES

Once a little girl,
                always my little girl
The moment I give your hand to
another man
                the way you look at
each other. I see your reflection in his clear,
bright pupils

your
                glittering round eyes behind
the white lace
                bridal gown
                with the same smile, you gave

                                                to me
seems like yesterday,
                when I first walked you to school
                                the same firm steps, you take

Once my little girl
                My daughter,
                                today is your big day.
But only a father can give a speech
                                with the weight
of a mixture
                                of tears and joy

Did you know?
        I once doubted and doubted
if today would   ever come
the fear was sometimes
            greater than all I have felt
            on the battlefield

My dear son-in-law,
        she's everything I have

May you live with happiness
    in life,
        together

    Always my
        little girl

If you ever get in a fight
with your husband

        Don't tell me about it
because
        you will end up forgiving him
I won't.

        Once a little girl,

           always my little girl.

To Children

You do not have to be innocent.
You do not have to crawl with bruised knees
all by yourself, through the dry cement road, begging.
You only have to spare attention to the inner child,
let yourself love what you love.

Over there, you will see the grass growing
away from the cracks on the road, reaching toward
its freedom,
waving at the sky with every cell it has.

It's wild out there, my children. Sometimes
hunters and the hunted exchange characters overnight.
Come home, come home. It does not matter who you are;
there is and will be a place for you, a unique soul like
yours.

History and the world will pass on,
your soul and mind will not.

Fences

Hug your kids
tell them you love them
because when thoughts become words,
words become actions, and that's when the
emotion will be transferred.

Spend time with your kids
earn less and hug more
even if that means struggling together.

Love your partner
because that is the best way
to teach someone how to respect and
to love and to be loved.

Write a letter and go to the post office
yourself and mail it out. Imagine the person
who receives the handwritten words and how
joyful their eyes would be.

Learn an instrument and learn a new language,
don't make excuses for having no time
when you have all the time to stay in the fences.

C'est la Vie

It's sunny here, half of me

It's rainy there, half of you

Writing is exchanging a part of
my soul with another soul

It is connecting with the unknown
and embracing the upcoming fear.

What is left
is what needs to be found
and to be defined
again.

Give me a flying penguin

Let's travel to Antarctica to find
a flying penguin, the type that has shiny eyes
and will only choose one partner for the rest of his life.

Let's interview the flying penguin
what it's like to create a family for himself
and to stay faithful despite the tragedy in his offspring.

Let's have dinner with the flying penguin
and catch some fish for each other
as a social gathering tradition at the dinner table.

Let's be like a flying penguin
without worries
only to go forward,
forward.

When losing becomes necessary

When you complain about a person you love,
your real thought of the person shifts to hatred
without recognizing it, like moments before the last road
lamp running out of light, leaving you to a nightmare,
and slowly drifting to a realistic feeling of disgust,
hiding behind all the meaningless conversations.

I will read a poem to you

Hey,

Science and math are important,
but humanity and art are what makes a person
different from the twenty-first century robots

If society needs calculating to function,
the human body needs the occasional, unique, inner
sparks
within them to live

*What is something you deeply believe in and when you
do it, you stop noticing the passing time?*

With full honesty,
make this one and only life
disturbingly surprising
foolishly courageous
dramatically classic.

Take a risk, join the game
Do what makes your heart come alive.

Name

Call someone by their name;
it is the best compliment you
can ever give.

Their Existence

thirty years later
they will not be here,
drinking the glass of water
while nagging you to clean the room

thirty years later
they will not be here,
comparing your success
to the "supposed to"

thirty years later
they will not be here,
dragging your emotions
away from sanity of the ordinary-looking daily life

thirty years later
they will become the "used to be"
and you will regret the
"could have been"

The girl dreams of

the misunderstanding to be misunderstood.
Climbing across the midnight classroom floor,
all the way to the blackboard with formulas written,
trying to calculate one brain's tolerance of another brain.

learn, break, get hurt, get up, trust, and again
learn, break, get hurt, get up, trust.

How to be alone and not feel lonely,
is the biggest battle you will need to go through
in order to grow.

If you happen to come across

me, searching for you in the
street full of mice and garbage.
You will see me there, kneeling and
begging a truth to be seen and to be valued.

If you happen to be running over her,
the veins will be full of blessing and regrets
all at once after eating too many disappointments
of the people's faces on the television and the news.

If you happen to be stepping over him,
the shouting and chanting will make you wonder
if this is the right thing to do, something in you
will realize the important, unspoken words in silence.

If you happen to be here,
you will know.

If you see me,
you will know.

Freeway of Happiness

Finding those everyone wanted will not make
you happy, because the best for you is not
necessarily the best for him, for her, and for them
the suitable ones are what you look for
when you need a source of happiness.

Love is to choose you again every day

It is a choice to stay
by the person every day
one day after another.

Seeing the time running
away while the reflection follows from
the old hanging wooden clock
wall, table, and to the dining room

Walking side-by-side with you in the supermarket
looking for the spices and ingredients for our dinner
instead of sitting across in formal dress
in a classy French restaurant

Love is to choose you again
every day. It goes beyond time zone,
distance, temperature, and ethnicity.

I will still choose you, again,
tomorrow.

Part 3

Say No Sometimes, Be Kind All Times

Door

It all started with

"Don't open the door,"
they said.

We became more curious
about the world
behind

the door.

11.24.18

Sitting on a ripped blanket that is full of little needles
There is something within your physical shell

A blurb of strings tightening your bones and organs
Pulling and destroying and loosening

All at once. The food debris along with their distorted
faces
"for our children, for our future," they shout once again

As you take a remote control and shut down
The media. The channel. The conversation. The body.

You realize the shivering in the air particles can't stop
The nails sink into the palm of your hand and made a
mark

Witness the white smoke coming out of their mouths blur
Your colors. Your hopes. Your vision. Your life.

We lost another young soul in the name of democracy
Do not ever forget, when the world quiets down

It is love that matters. It is love, that matters.
Do not ever forget, when the world quiets down

Take a seat, we still hold the ticket to the final destination
Do not ever forget, when the world quiets down

—

Written after Taiwan's election day on Nov. 24, 2018

Proud of You

"I am proud of you."
The world's most oppressive combination
of
five simple words.

Honor, it was and
it should have been.

Arrogance, it became
as the emotions tangle up in your mouth,
when you throw up along with
useless pride that is tied in
with your favorite ribbon.

"I am proud of you."
Make me say this, please.
Try, try, try harder.

Guilt, it was not and
should not have been.

A tool to look better, if you
get a smaller copy of yourself
with failed, distrusted DNA
use it well.

Shame, it was not
but was, for you.

"I am proud of you."

The beginning of the end that
destroys many souls.

The Repeated

I'm the type of person who
knows the movie has a 32% rating
on Rotten Tomatoes
and still insists on watching it.

Who are they, the middle-aged couple
living across from my house,
When they wake up in the morning
She stares blankly at him, while
He always put the white daffodil
On her right ear

The center of the white petals,
Wrinkling like some parts of her skin,
Her hair dancing through the
Blue summer breeze, along with the
Old school jazz by Charlie Parker in the house

Their red-shuttered windows are always open,
The wooden frame outside is almost rotten,
The red is like the color in her eyes when she
Stays up looking at the daffodil through the
Slanted oval-shaped mirror

He removes the daffodil from her ear,
as if he's getting rid of a flea from a stray dog.
She looks into his eyes through the reflection,
Then the bedroom light is off.

The next morning, the daffodil petals

are spread into an oval shape
with a red wax candle in front of my door,
"You're next," the note reads.

A Song to the Misguided Soul

Somewhere, someone's inner potential
to commit a crime is to twist
where the social consciousness is going.

Committing it with silence
Committing it with no actions
Committing it with a smiley mask

Tick, tock! Tick, tock!
I will not wish you a good evening with a good
night's sleep;
I will wish you courage and a pair of clear eyes
to see through the lies wrapped carefully in a surprise box.

The Same

Find those who
>appreciate the handwritten letters
>remember your favorite food
>value your existence and well-being
>understand the importance of timing
>walk on the same path as you

Find those who
>bring you positive vibes
>make you want to be a better person
>cherish your hard work and dedication
>help you recognize who you are
>direct you when you need guidance

Be with people like you

Don't force it, never force it.

What do you want to be when you grow up

I pick up a pen,
instead of a surgical mess.
I cut through each and every character's
life story and brain structure,
peeking through the painful and the wonderful.

I pick up a book,
instead of a chemical tube.
I read through the wrongs and the unjust
believing the possibility in creating new history
bringing a light through the cracks in the corruption.

I pick up a leaf,
outside of the small town library.
singing along with the spring breeze,
secretly promising to chase after another leaf
despite seeming like a fool in a crowd of the bravest
humans.

I pick up myself,

pick up the
role
as a storyteller.

Their own happiness

It is as if someone forces you to volunteer,
to be choked with a cheap red plastic bag.
Making the love of your life stare into
your fearless soul, stepping into the entrance
door of the seven sins you were accused of.

This happens if you allow them to.
You allow yourself to experience and to take in
the pain and grief.

People could be bad. They feed on someone's
unhappiness for their own happiness.

Take what you want away,
leave a piece of you here.

Rich men's dream

When you believe you have everything
a person ever wanted, that usually means
you have nothing.

When you value someone's opinion more than
your own, that means you are losing
yourself as a young child.

We can only call ourselves
mature souls when we accept the uncertainty
and to live with fear of the unknown.

I'll shower with you in the rain

Dear,

I can't stop the rain in the city for you,
but I am willing to send you a raincoat
and fly there to be with you.

I can't tell your supervisor to raise
your salary or pay your bills for you,
but I can fight at your side when you are treated unfairly.

I can't make him come back in your life,
and I can't replace who he was to you,
but I can listen and be here with you.

I can't take away all the pain from sickness;
I am not God and I can't bring back the lost,
but I can promise you are not along in this journey.

I can't stop the rain for you;
I will stand in the rain with you.

Definition of Success

What is your definition of success?
Earning lots of money and buying everything
you've ever wanted?

I have lost my mind when confronted with this question.

We are too young to be thinking about success.
We are too old to be thinking about success.

Success, you are what you claim you are.

Live quietly, create with a loud mind—
that's my type of success.

Pink is not the girl

When you were born, they said to buy a pink bracelet for the baby girl. They said to also put a lace ribbon in your hair, and they called you a little princess. They bought you the pinkest hot pink tutu dress to match the ribbon. Your pink life started. You waited to be fed by the pink spoon with the character wearing a pink dress like yours on it. You grew to believe the pink and those beliefs that were fed into you. You know pink and you learn to not know pink.

Motions

It takes a life-and-death situation
for people to break the motion.

Family is like breathing:
you will never see one's value
until you are running out of breath,
choking, in pain, struggling to live.

Family is like a string of Christmas lights,
gathered together with too many hopes
and expectations of one another,
dragging the entire tree down.

Family is the box of rotten milk stored in the
corner of your fridge that causes disruption;
you should throw it away when it's passed the date
but still cannot get the courage to do it.

Let the bird sing

Don't force your children to learn
piano and expect them to grow up
and become a gentle adult due to
the musical influence from a poor,
dying musician from the eighteenth century.

Don't organize the music sheets in order
while wiping off the dust from the names
and think they will make a song out of
themselves when there is no practice
of your fingers reading through them.

Don't beat the young souls because
they run away from the chair in front
of a black monster making noise in the middle of
classy living room, just so you can feel proud
and accomplished by its existence and ability to shout.

The bird sings the loudest when
no one is watching.

Good Temper, Bad Temper

One moment in time,
your pupil is no longer clear like water; instead it is gray
and turbid.

One moment in time,
your emotions are covered with
politeness under the social structure.

One moment in time,
you're shocked by your own
temper—slow, steady, and firm

Walking on the path of flowers
looking forward to another
growth.

Reversible

Waking up early in the morning is like being in an abusive relationship,
Being in an abusive relationship is like drowning in your
sixth-grade swimming class,
Drowning in your sixth-grade swimming class is like farting while giving a speech,
Farting while giving a speech is like having red lipstick
smeared on your teeth on the first date,
Having red lipstick smeared on your teeth on the first date
is like Disneyland without Mickey Mouse,
Disneyland without Mickey Mouse is like a childhood
without the cartoon channel,
A childhood without the cartoon channel is like getting
rejected by your crush at high school prom,
Getting rejected by your crush at high school prom is like
submitting the wrong resume to the wrong company,
Submitting the wrong resume to the wrong company is
like waking up early in the morning.

My Dear

Don't bring the sadness and anger from your
original family to the future family you are about to
create with the person you love.

Dear,
listen to what's missing in the family
meeting.

Dear,
look for the absence and silence
in the conversation.

Dear,
watch for who is speaking with
sincerity.

You have every right to be angry
when someone is crossing the line.

Passing By

I watched the movie you recommended,
but I didn't go back and watch the clips we
filmed when we were still together.

Sometimes, time is like an old roll of film:
when it's extended, you get to see which
segments are necessary and which are not.

Keep those that are important under the light,
leave those that are extra in the dark room.

Checklist

Go see the person you miss
tell the soul everything you feel
as soon as you see them

Give a hug to the one next to you
who is often forgotten when life gets busy
and days become nights

Leave some time for yourself to
recharge, doing everything you used to love
as a child in your early memories

Pay attention to the details like
how someone makes you feel around them
instead of what is said and what you're told

See the world like it's your last time in life
to find broken lines and the balance in
between the gray, the uneven, and the ugly

Those who point at you

If you consider yourself young,
don't hesitate to take care of yourself
both physically and mentally

If you consider yourself old,
don't hesitate to slow down because
of what limits you and what others say

If you consider yourself lost in between,
pick the pieces that remind you of you
back up, and restart the journey anytime

Don't lock yourself in the
cycle of time when you could embrace
the differences in the upcoming great unknown

Part 4

Fight Like a Warrior

God, Make Me a Kinder Person

Make me a kinder person,
The one person who puts the plastic bottles in the right
recycling bin with
confidence & without looking at the example of what's
supposed to go in,
& gladly does so for another person even when he is not
looking.

Make me a kinder person,
Who considers the passenger sitting next to me & doesn't
move to
another side of the bus where there are two empty seats,
especially when
all you hear is air breaks & the driver starts talking about
his personal life.

Make me a kinder person,
Who doesn't go on social media & spam my best friend
about how bad
today's traffic is & how the line at the supermarket is long
& dry when
the chubby lady's kid with curly hair won't stop crying in
front of me.

Make me a kinder person,
So I can imagine myself in my neighbor's wrinkling bull-
dog's shoes &
see why it's necessary for him to drool & pee on my wool
rug in front of
my door every time he takes a walk past.

Make me a kinder person,
& make me not question why there can't be more people
like me who show they care
when I actually care, & be okay with the unkind soul in
me, all to find
a way to still live on with the minimum wage of kindness.

SONNET OF A TRUTHFUL LIE

The mottled yellow wall starts falling apart like
your layered white lies, as spicy as raw onions.
They say the real bad people don't lie, the ones who lie
are bad people who want to be good people.
It all started small. Everything always starts small like
your lie about the snowball slowly falls from the tallest
hill in the coldest place on the earth.
The truth is your snowball of words are frozen and will
always be.
Poetry is different though, they say. Whatever pain or
retrospective
moments of truth you feel here are real and always will be.
When it's you and silence left in that white room with
no windows,
promise me you will be good people speaking to bad lies.
Believe the lie, you will be harmed.
Live the truth, you will be healed.

A Purpose

Listen, to what is left
when the city quiets down.

To be a writer
Does not mean
To pour
A plot;

The twist
Is not
Complex
Nor is it
Sleeping

Seek, yes
Thriving, yes

Living in its time;

Yes.

Yes.

My Angel Hero

This poem is for you.

"Don't be your biggest enemy."
She was a friend and a teacher.

At the age of fifteen,
to have met someone
who trusts you
with all the patience in the world,
who believes in you after all the wrongful
accusations
in your life.

At the age of fifteen,
the most confusing stage between
a teenager and an adult,
inner stirring soul conflicts with
outer stiffer shells, all under
one little body and being told,
"It's okay."

At the age of fifteen,
you blame yourself for everything,
the person who took away your
favorite bunny and who threatened to
burn your holiday sweater given as a gift.
You blame, you still do.
a hundred souls locked in place.

I might not have grown to become a great adult,

but I am now a kind person to
myself and to the world.

Thank you, thank you.

I love you, so you need to love yourself

Thank you for reminding me
to love again as I am loved
by you

"I love you,
so you need to love yourself"

Sometimes all you need is
not a promise, you need
"I'll be there," knowing
all the forces behind you
even if you fail miserably.

List of Dreams

1. To have perfect eyesight again
2. To not worry about the feeling of worrying
3. To write a poem for every single person on this planet
4. To always have a heart hoping for the best despite seeing the worst
5. To not know the future and accept the unknowns
6. To fall asleep naturally without a fear of darkness
7. To use money wisely and not being controlled by the numbers
8. To believe a dream will always be a sweet one and not a nightmare
9. To be okay reading a story without a clear resolution
10. To cut down the list of dreams and focus on what's more important

Prescription

1. Hug your favorite teddy bear three times with all the energy you have.
2. Go see the one person on your mind you can't live without.
3. Take a day off because you need a mental health day for yourself.
4. Lie on the bed and feel the blankets wrap around every inch of your skin.
5. Stop whatever you are thinking. Leave the thoughts for later.
6. You will recover. You will be fine.

One Day

The concrete fact is that
time is a thief,
stealing the permanent forever

Romanticizing every dream
Of
Ours

I've always gotten an
obsessed satisfaction
from crossing dates off
my calendar

Thinking
In the enormous universe
To have met you,
How amazing

Like fireworks
Mixture of passionate red
With depressing blue
Short but marvelous

The spark was the love constant
Something that I thought
was either
Zero
or
One

To the one person who made me believe I deserve the entire world

To like is to
remember his favorite flavor of ice cream
To love is to
give him the only scoop of ice cream you have

To like is to
only want to be with him at this moment
To love is to
choose to be with him every day from now on

To like is to
share the enjoyable things in life with him
To love is to
take on the good and bad in life together

To like is to
laugh with him on the brightest days
To love is to
stay with him on the darkest sleepless nights

To like, to: like
To love, to: love

To Heal

You do not need to buy a first-class plane ticket,
fly to the busiest city with a luggage full of dreams,
emerge yourself in a Broadway show, and expect the
good-looking stranger sitting next to you to heal you.

You do not need the twenty-four-inch waist and to buy
the newest collection from the luxurious, fashionable
lingerie store to feel like you deserve to be loved as a
woman and hope others' looks of envy will heal your
never-ending sickness.

You do not need to be drowning in cash at the end of
every month from your long, boring day job just so
your parents can tell their friends you are a good child
who makes your family proud, so you can heal everyone.

Trust
you can make the right decision
under every difficult moment
even it means to go against what is
expected.

Every Reason

Listen,
you have every reason to be mad when you are.

Do not
hide your emotions and bury your tears
Do not
shut your mouth just to listen to others
Do not
make yourself unhappy by pretending to like others
Do not
disrespect every mood of yours when it clearly exists
Do not
lock yourself in the room when you want to exit

Every reason to be / you

Have every reason to
be upset, disappointed, angry

Face it,
so you can still be
you.

Translator for Mother

"I'm not hungry; you should eat it."
Your hunger upsets me. I will give mine to you.

"I am not cold. Put my jacket on."
I am worried about you catching a cold in this weather.

"Are you coming home this weekend?"
Your father and I miss you. Come home to see us.

"I don't need gifts on my birthday. Use your money
on yourself."
I am happy that you remember my birthday.

"Don't worry, I'm not sleepy. I will watch TV while waiting
for you."
I want to make sure you get home safely.

"I love you."
I love you.

Love is to travel with you

Walking side by side, and
holding your hands tighter in a crowded
Christmas market in Vienna.

Buying you your favorite London log
flavor ice cream in a waffle cone on a hot
summer day in Rome.

Taking photos of you wearing a kimono with a pink
ribbon when the spring breeze flows through your
long hair in front of the red Kyoto shrine.

Humming the same song with you when
lining up for Hawaiian shaved ice in your swimsuits
next to the Waikiki beach.

Lying down with you on the hot summer grass
in front of the Eiffel Tower, watching another
couple taking their wedding photoshoot.

Smiling at each other and planning to
explore and to start another adventure
together, somewhere in the world.

Speak with your eyes

Give me the look you have when
you are determined that you know the correct
answer to the question being asked in class

Show me the eyes you have when
you talk about something you love and your
pupils dilate as if you saw a shooting star

Bring me the best version you have of yourself when
you strongly believe in what you look for
after every careful decision made

my dear, the power comes after
what you believe shines through
in your eyes

Far away from home

That's where I am from.

The distance between me and my family
is one ocean across.
My kindergarten teacher told me that
parents' love is as deep as the ocean
and they will do things like climb
to the rocky surface of the moon
to bring me back the brightest star.

But no one ever wondered how deep the ocean is
or figured out a way to measure someone's
capacity to love and to be loved.

Would you still love the way I am even if I was not
related to you at all?

Would you value my values as a human being?

Would you respect my type of home and be proud of it?

People talk about how love wins at the end of every story,
but they never talk about the regrets and sacrifices behind
those seemingly good endings.

Are you home?

I'm on my way.

He, She, You, Me

Blaming one and the other
is contagious.

People are like ants, except
we work the best when the goal is to
avoid responsibilities.

It's like playing the musical chairs.
No one will save a seat for you
when it has to do with their chance of survival.

Fight for you,
yourself.

You only have this life.

The path

Dear,
this is a path you must walk
let the world misunderstand you
let the people judge
let the noises be
as long as you are
on the path to be
you.

1, 2, 3

Don't settle for being okay.
Strive for the best.

Don't let go of the "what if"s.
Fight for the "can be"s.

Don't lose to the fear.
Be prepared to be scared.

Little ones,
Ask all the questions.

Ask on,
Find out how to find out.

A cup of time

We, humans, beings
are the only animals
who lock ourselves in the zone of time.

It's 11 a.m. I have another forty minutes
to finish another three tasks with two coworkers.

Hey,
I want to buy away your unhappiness.
I want to buy away your time with a cup of coffee
that I believe is more worthy than your time spent on
things
that will no longer matter in five years but caused you a
head full of gray hair.

Time's up.
How much do you charge?

The Good in You

What was your reaction when you first
found out Santa on Christmas Eve was
paid by your dad to deliver the gift he
got the night before at Target?

What was on your mind when you first
voted for someone because of his honesty
then were cheated when none of what he
said came true for the city?

What was your intention when you wished
a stranger a nice day, though you
just wanted them to leave you alone because
you just lost your day job?

What was on your mind when the
city in your eyes was full of colors and
possibilities, like a childhood playground
with every adventure you were ready to explore?

Untitled

It is only when what you love and who you love
are challenged, that you realize
how much they mean and how much
space they take up in your heart.

I will be there for you

Rain or shine,
the world tomorrow will go on.

It will not care whether you lose
the love of your life, or if you win the
biggest lottery in the city.

Chain of events,
let them happen.

Love Is To Be Loved

What is the perfect season to be loved?
And meet someone to save you from the dark,
A lifetime season, oh my dear beloved
Our story now starts from the moment spark.
Yet we treasure, direction of His will,
O what a great mercy, the gift from Him.
Until the life journey goes down to hill—
I wot life without thee is space of dim
Love me and I will give it all to thou,
Thy tongue, thy lips as sweet as thy sugar
See seasons change, everyday with thou
And year after year, this will be forever.
      Spring breeze, hot sun, fall leaves, cold night
with thou,
      White dress on me to make thy dream come true.

Part 5

Finale—Not the End

ABOUT REGRETS

I wonder what would have happened if I just let myself sink into the six-meter-deep pool when you pushed me in. People said drowning hurts and your body becomes swollen if no one finds you for hours, or for several days. *I don't want to die ugly*, so I forced myself out of the consciousness. There were people I could've saved, there were circumstances in which I could've done something, and there were confessions I could've made. However, I was always too afraid. Past, present, and future—I want to be responsible for myself. *Be kind and try to live without regrets*, I tell myself. The days that are about to come are composed of every little decision you make now and those you made in the past.

ABOUT LOVE

I never believed things like "true love" or "love at first sight."
Anyone can be anyone's first choice of love and last choice, of
course. It is never about the time. It has always been about
how much two people are willing to lock themselves in a
space together with an open door. People read too many
articles on "five signs a man loves you" and take too many
online quizzes on "best type of women for you." We want
everything to be so fast in our generation. And we forget,
or choose to forget, some things are faster when we do
them slower.

Humans are funny. We are the animals that limit ourselves with watches, clocks, time frames, and restrictions. Older humans tell me: "You will understand everything the moment before you die." Why wait that long to cherish? I could never answer for them. There is a reason we don't know when our last moment will be. There is a reason we can't keep memories with us after we pass on. There is a reason no one has come back and tell us what the end of the life journey looks like. There is always a reason.

ABOUT LIFE

There is a gray area in everything. You are going to feel pain, hurt, abandonment in many different ways. What is the point of life? I'm too young to answer this and too old to answer this. All I know is: pay attention to the details. The little moments are what days and months are made of. The little moments like the angle of his smile or your daily routine with her are what you will remember when people ask you about those years. There are shadows underneath the trees. There is a brief summer breeze when you lie in the park with her. Those years, there is you and me. The combination of those seemingly boring details is what I call romantic about one's life.

Was a storyteller. Am a storyteller. Will always be a story-teller. I wish I could physically come out of the book and give you a hug. I could not attach a hug in the price of the book you pay for. It is priceless, just like all the valuable things in your life. Whether today was a good day or a bad day for you, remember you still got yourself at the end of the day. If lost, pause and find yourself again. If life does not treat you well at this moment, pause and hold on to what makes you feel alive. Be patient and be open with options. If you remember nothing else from the book, please remember everyone deserves to be loved. You deserve the best. Dear, may your life be filled with love.

Work Referenced

"Taiwan voters reject same-sex marriage in referendums." *BBC News*. 25 November 2018. https://www.bbc.com/news/world-asia-46329877.

Walter, Mischel. *The Marshmallow Test*. Transworld Digital, 2014

Acknowledgements

Lloyd Alexander once said all that writers can do is keep trying to say what is deepest in their hearts. I believe I have said mine. I am ready to accept the consequences and pressure, for my texts being who they need to be.

I imagine many people tend to skip this section of the book. So, if you are still here, thank you, for reading my adventure, my secrets, and my poetry. There are people in my life who I must thank and include.

"Why don't you write a book?" he asked. I told him an opportunity to publish a book is not what you get every day. This conversation had kept me awake on many nights before I met my publisher and the team. There were times I did not think I was ready. The person who helped me overcome my anxiety, who proved me to be braver than I imagined, and who pushed me to question what it meant to be a writer was Han Kyou Choi. Thank you, James, for everything.

I remember my best friend called me on the phone when she faced challenges and doubted herself. I shared my beliefs with her and told her how much I believe in her even when life gets difficult. She told me "I wish someone could write a book that includes what you just said." I then gained some confidence to write about my experience and my views on relationships, life, and time. Here it is, June Park. Thank you for teaching me to be stubborn when it comes to protecting my dream.

I was afraid to write out some of the contents in this book of poetry because it could get so personal and I could break-down while writing it. "Don't let that stop you!" The person who encouraged me to keep going was Emi Gilbert. Emi is intelligent, thoughtful, and a cat lover who I always enjoy spending time with. Every conversation with you could inspire me to write another poem. Thank you for being my strongest support system.

This book would not have been here without Professor Eric Koester. Thank you for answering my questions and providing me detailed feedback. I would like to thank the team at New Degree Press. Special thanks to Brian Bies and Leila Summers. My editors Clayton Bohle, Elina Oliferovskiy, and Catriona Kendall have made suggestions that helped me to improve as a writer. Thank you for working with me despite different time zones. As a designer myself, picking a cover was more difficult than I imagined it to be. Thank you, Aleksandra Dabic for working with me and designing the lovely cover!

Also thank you to everyone who: gave me their time for a personal interview, pre-ordered the eBook, paperback, and multiple copies to make publishing possible, helped spread the word about *REBORN* to gather amazing momentum, and help me publish a book I am proud of. Celine Yu, Charlotte Lin, Chun Hung Chiu, Donna Lee Crewe, Emi

Gilbert, Evelyn Chiaen Ho, Giselle Wyers, Han Kyou Choi, Hung Pi Chih Chiu, Johan Hurtada Velo, Joshua Lee, Josiah Sum, June Park, Kevin Lin, Ling Ling Chiu, Lyn Lin, Maggie Wang, Shih Shin-di, Shu Fang Jan, Ta Pang Chiou, Tony Chiu, Venus Su, Ying Ho Chou, and many many more. I am sincerely grateful for all of your help.

And to everyone on Facebook and Instagram who has helped to share my book, especially the posts under #ahcpoetry and #aeimee. Thank you!

Thank you foremost to my family for supporting me through every step of the way, always. Fulfilling this dream would not have been possible without you. Thank you, Dad, Mom, Tony, and Linda. I love you all.

Author Bio

 How better to get to know a person than read their innermost thoughts? Meet Amy Hsuan Chiu, poet, artist, designer, polyglot and bunny doll collector. She turns her daily emotions into poetry to be shared with others, displays her artwork at shows around town, speaks four languages (and is learning a fifth), and refuses to grow up. Chiu loves reminiscing about her childhood memories in Hawaii and staying up all night writing — or, as she puts it, being "swallowed up by the written words." Chiu believes that poetry is a deeply personal experience; something she uses to heal from certain emotions and as a way to deal with various difficulties. In her first book, *REBORN: To Heal. To Believe. To Love.*, Chiu explores the merging of darkness vs. light and reality vs. dream. The author faces each day with a smile and each person with a friendly greeting. Her outgoing nature and people skills have helped her adapt to the fluctuations of life. Graduating from the University of Washington with degrees in Creative Writing and Visual Arts, Ms Chiu has now turned attention to travel; seeking international inspiration.

www.ingramcontent.com/pod-product-compliance
Lightning Source LLC
Chambersburg PA
CBHW071524180526
45171CB00002B/376